PAUL BIRTILL

NEW AND
SELECTED POEMS

Hearing Eye

Published by Hearing Eye 2016

Reprinted with revisions 2017

Hearing Eye, Box 1, 99 Torriano Avenue
London NW5 2RX, UK
email: hearing_eye@torriano.org
www.hearingeye.org

—∞—

ISBN 9781905082742

ACKNOWLEDGEMENTS

Some of these poems first appeared in the following publications: *The Guardian,
The Independent, Daily Express, Morning Star, Liverpool Daily Post, Irish Post, The
Spectator, New Statesman, The Author, London Magazine, Outposts, Acumen, The
Rialto, The North, Smiths Knoll, The SHOp, Orbis, The Interpreter's House, Poetry
and Audience, The Wolf, Envoi, Poetry Nottingham, The Frogmore Papers, Spokes,
The Echo Room, Scratch, Pennine Platform, Rising, Psychopoetica, Braquemard,
Gargoyle, Brixton Poets, 14, Pen Pusher, The Alarmist, Shrike, The Eggbox, Ape,
Trespass, South Bank Poetry, Aisle 16, The Liberator, Still, Poetry Seen, Poetry
Street, The Delinquent, Krax, Poetry On The Buses, Poetry On The Internet,* were
included in the anthologies: *Velocity, In The Company Of Poets, Oral, Saltpetre,
Out From Beneath The Boot, Poems For The Retired Nihilist, The Real Survivors,
In Dark Times, Well Versed, The Dead Good Poets Society,* and were broadcast on:
BBC Radio Merseyside, BBC Radio 4, BBC London Live, Resonance FM, Express
FM, Radio 100 Amsterdam, and were featured in films made by students of the
London International Film School, by Ben Gregor, and by Omnia Films.

Trade distribution: Central Books Ltd,
50 Freshwater Road, Chadwell Heath, London RM8 1RX

Designed by Martin Parker at www.silbercow.co.uk
Printed by Catford Print Centre, London SE6 4PY

CONTENTS

New Poems

KEEPING WATCH

There is a history of insanity
in that family going back three
generations and they watch each
other like hawks for signs.
They are over-controlled in that house
impulsive behaviour is non-existent.
I stayed there once and nobody
laughed shouted sang cried or
did anything emotional they just
watched – they watched each other
like hawks for signs and
one said as I was leaving,
'It's in our genes you know.'

CHEATING DEATH

No ambulance siren
No audience or crowd
No morbid doctor with
shocking diagnosis
No months of pain
and messing the bed
No operating theatres
or cream painted wards
just two hundred tranquillisers
and a room by the sea
Oh yes it's Hastings for me.

79 KINGFIELD

There wasn't much room
in our house so I crashed
in Ma's room 'til I was ten.

Sometimes she'd get up and
piss in an orange bucket.
Quite often she'd see something
and call out.
I hated the night.

Occasionally the old man
would creep in, tiptoe
past my bed and give
her one, unaware I was
awake listening.
They were both in their fifties.
I hated the night.

She became ill and
moaned with pain
throughout the night
getting up to take
pills walk about
and piss in the orange bucket.
The old man stopped coming.

When I was ten my
dad built an attic on
the roof and I got my own room,
small though it was,
the nights were peaceful.
I learnt to sleep.

PROBLEMS DESCRIBING
A DEAD PERSON

The argument was about
whether or not LOVING FATHER
should be inscribed on his
tomb and it raged for three
days and three nights with
short breaks for food. Many
a violent word was spoken
and at one point Fred said
he'd smash the grave with
a hammer. It was finally
resolved by a sensitive
neighbour who came up
with an acceptable compromise
SADLY MISSED BY SOME.

CHRISTMAS IN BEDSIT LAND

Christmas is coming
and there's a violent maniac
in the attic.
He keeps threatening to
come down and give me a
good hiding because I have
lots of callers and he has none.
I've told the landlady but
she sez she can't evict him
until he actually gives me
the hiding.
He sez he's gonna do it
right after the Queen's speech
and I believe him.

WAITING FOR MY MOTHER

Fifty-three and totally grey
wishing to avoid the
young mothers – was always
          last to arrive.
I could wait twenty minutes
and then, when the road was clear
in an old coat, looking tired
          and perhaps
          a little embarrassed
          she'd appear.
I was always pleased to see her –
well worth waiting for
was my old mum.

COUPLES

Couples are a nuisance
they're always waiting
for you to leave so they
can start mauling one another.
There's only me and this
fat kid with glasses left
in the village who haven't
got a girlfriend and he's
asked me to go on holiday;
everybody's watching us.

OUT WALKING WITH MY FATHER

That woman's got
cancer of the hand
it may spread
it may not.
That building's not safe
it's going to collapse
and kill people –
little children probably.
A man strangled
a woman in that
park last year.
That dog could
bite you and
give you rabies.
Watch a car
doesn't hit you
or you'll end up
with no legs.
Out walking with my father
the world became a terrifying place.

OBSESSIVE THINKER

He doesn't go to work
just lies on his bed
and thinks.
He reads no books and
writes no letters
just lies on his bed
and thinks.
In fact he has no hobbies
or interests except that
is to think.
He doesn't drink in company
prefers to drink and think.
He eats TV dinners – they're
quick an' easy to prepare
which means more time
to think.
He never goes to sleep at night
just lies there and thinks.
And what does he think about?
Whether or not he's having a good time.

WILL I BE ABLE TO DIE

Will I be able
to die
Do I have
what it takes
Do I have
the guts
Will I be able
to relax enough
when the time comes
– let go completely
or might I chicken
out at the last moment
and will the doctor
have to smother me with
a pillow – how humiliating.

LONER

He was so used to his own company
that whenever anyone
spoke to him – asked
him his name or how
he was feeling – assumed
for a moment he had just
been in a road accident and
they were trying to keep him alive.

SAD BASTARD

Wears shades to
hide the pain
health irrelevant
appearance unimportant
happiness not recalled
No-one likes a sad bastard.

Alone in a pub
not looking around
not interested
quite still
life's a chore
No-one likes a sad bastard.

Snivelling in a bedsit
eating beans from a can
ripping up suicide notes
watching a kids programme
No-one likes a sad bastard.

Shuffling through a park
having bitter thoughts
chucks stones at the ducks
shouts abuse at a squirrel
lies in the wet grass and cries
No-one wants a sad bastard.

Passes the Samaritans
on his way home
gives it two fingers
and starts to run
A sudden flash of courage
– he can do it,
this time it's for real
who'll miss a sad bastard.

STRANGERS ON A TUBE

He picked his nose
She laughed
He wiped it on her coat
She slapped his face
He head-butted her
I carried on reading Keats –
thank God for Poems on the Underground.

THE MAN WHO COULDN'T CHANGE

He watched his sister change
many times during her breakdown
so equated it with madness
and, like a dead tree, for
fifteen years forced himself
to stay and be exactly the same;
in case they should send
him to the asylum too.

BITTER OLD FART

I didn't smoke
and now I'm deaf

didn't drink
now I'm incontinent

didn't have late nights
now I'm senile

didn't eat junk food
yet I can hardly see

didn't take drugs
yet I ache all over

didn't laze about
yet I'm stuck in this chair

didn't get fat
now I've shrunk

didn't take risks
now I stink the
place out

didn't overspend
now I'm poor

I never really enjoyed myself
like other people but they're
all dead, and I'm alone.

THE SHED

I watched the new tenants
pull down the old shed on Sunday afternoon
and remembered the day it was first
erected, some twenty years ago.
It took half an hour to dismantle
yet had taken the Gunnings' two
sons, Francis and Arthur, most of
an afternoon to build. Their parents
who were on holiday at the time
had been pestering them to put one
up for months, and I think it was
meant as a surprise. When they
had finished they began to argue
and then fight. I shouted
at them both to stop as they rolled around
the lawn exchanging blows and screaming
at one another, but they took no notice.
Then Arthur grabbed a hammer and walloped
Francis several times over the head with it
– he later died in hospital. The Gunnings
returned home the next day to discover they'd
gained a shed and lost a son.

BODY TALK

I hate my body
and it hates me
I fill it with tar
and tons of ale
it responds with
horrible pains
We have no respect
for one another
we give each other hell.

I exercise it rarely
and feed it some
awful shit
it retaliates with more
horrible pains
What a carry on.

Soon we'll part company
and the fighting will end
but not before it puts
me through agony for the
years I've mistreated it
horrible bloody thing.

REINCARNATION

Is this ladybird
Sir Oswald Mosley
Is this cockroach
Sir Stafford Cripps
Is this beetle
Pitt the younger
Is my cat
Heydrich 'the hangman'
I'll boot its arse
just in case.

NERVOUS TWITCH

Can you imagine anything more unfashionable
than an uncontrollable nervous twitch like
shaking your head or blinking your eyes for
instance. I often wonder about twitches and
how disastrous it would be to develop one.
I sit in my executive chair and shudder at
the thought of shaking my head down at the
club or screwing up my face hideously at a
dinner party – I'd lose all my social status
in one twitch. I might even become an outcast
if it got bad enough – a laughing-stock for sure.
Sometimes I stand in front of the mirror
do a few little twitches and then run to the
drinks cabinet and pour myself a large whisky.

FATHER-IN-LAW

He didn't like the mechanic
who wanted the daughter he
fancied but after a fight
gave her away. They moved
next door and now both men
enjoy a pint together on
Sundays, talk about sex and
work under the car.

VEGETARIAN

I wish I was a vegetarian
sometimes, then I could
boil a potato and eat it
with a stupid smile on my face.

ME TOO

Some of these poets
have big ideas especially
after they've had a few beers
– imagine they'll be read
in a hundred years!

AFFECTION

Couldn't show it
didn't know it
thought it was
a diseased condition.
Such a shame
no-one to blame.

WAKING UP

Last night I dreamt
I was a child again
playing by a stream.

Last night I dreamt
I was on holiday and
fell in love.

Last night I dreamt
it was my twenty-first
birthday and I was very
drunk.

This morning I awoke in
my hospital bed remembered
I was dying and cried.

STINKIN' PARTY

Flirting with an assortment of sheer rubbish
exchanging lines with smiling enthusiasts
thirsting for dialogue.
A hundred or so bloody good moods
crammed into a noisy little room.
Half dancing rotating heads scouting
for a spouse to spend half a century with.
Excited enough to wet your pants like a
dog that's been chained up for a week.
Burying one's liquor in the garden to
ensure drunkenness throughout.

Bell warns of new arrivals with fresh dialogue.
But why should I converse with these keen
sparkling hyped-up shit-bags who've been
ignoring me on the underground all week.
Giving them the attention reserved for dying relatives,
they'll not get a peep out of me.

Wish I was the gatecrasher who treads
dog muck into every carpet, nicks a few ornaments,
– fucks off early.

Those with style, superior lines and an
above average jig end up in a room fit
for pigs spending the remainder of the
night rolling round a cold floor
touching up several stone of unfamiliar
foul-smelling flesh.

They take it to a bit of green
the next day, clutch its grubby
hand like they've known it for years –
make arrangements for a weekend by the sea.

Eighty per cent of accidents
occur in the home, why can't
we see a few at parties.

GOD WORKS IN MYSTERIOUS WAYS

Aberfan, Multiple Sclerosis
Spastics and the Somme
Bloody mysterious.

Cancer, Culloden
Famine and President Botha
Weird.

Motorway pile-ups
Cot-deaths and Hiroshima
A trifle peculiar.

Schizophrenia, Zeebrugge
Thatcherism and Belsen
Damn strange.

Aids and Ulster
Strokes, Cardboard City
and of course the
human being.

Is he worth an hour
on Sunday?
Surely not.

PRIEST WITHOUT A HEAD

When I was a child
I used to dream a lot
of headless priests
coming towards me in
their silk vestments –
arms stretched out.
My dad told me seeing
the priest without a
head meant that I would
lose my faith as an adult.
Some years later our parish
priest lost his head in a car crash.

TRAGIC SMELL

The whisky
on your breath
smells horrible.
It smells of domestic
violence deprived children
and good friends lost forever.

The whisky
on your breath
is making me sick.
It smells of corruption
in low places the theft
of fifteen pounds a cheap
affair and losing at the races.

The smell of whisky on your breath
makes me quite depressed.

SO MANY WAYS TO DIE

So obsessed with death
in all its forms – he
wanted to die not once
but a thousand times –
trying every single cause
of death known to man.
How frustrating he thought
that a person could only
die of one ailment. However
he was comforted by the fact
there may be complications.

AIM LOW SCORE HIGH

Whilst trying
to emulate Jesus Christ
I lost all my friends
and got my head kicked
in four times.
My mate on the other hand
who was inspired by King
Herod in his early teens
seems to be having a ball
of a time – everybody loves him.
I might have a crack at Bonaparte
when I leave hospital.

FALLING IN SHIT

A certain smile
or silly look
An accent or a laugh
some hackneyed phrase
or witty one liner
I'm falling in shit.

A piece of cabbage
between the teeth
A raincoat soaked through
tripping in the street
dropping an ice cream
nearly choking on a fishbone
I'm falling in shit.

A cut finger
some burnt sausages
An unusual gift
a thoughtful gesture
A birthmark, plaster
pattern on a jumper
I'm falling in shit.

Some angry exchanges
a button coming off a shirt
a sad tale.
A bit of eccentricity
a minimum of defects
– possibly going places
I've fallen in shit.

WORK-SHY WRITER

You get lazy people
in any field, I write poems
instead of novels. You start
at nine and finish at half
past and have the rest of
the day to yourself – money's
crap though.

SMOKING IN BED

I always have a cigarette
last thing
I turn out the light
lie back and spark up
I love to smoke in bed.

Often I wake up
with my quilt on fire
or the ashtray over my head.
There are holes in my
pillow and sheets
but I love to smoke
in bed.

One day the whole
house will go up
and there are kiddies
in the flat above.
But I don't give
a monkey's
I love to smoke
in bed.

FEMINIST

If I were a feminist
I should prefer a
bible-thumping misogynist
to a liberated male
who changes one in
ten nappies and lets
me go to my night-class
on Thursdays.

PESTERING THE DOCTOR

I rang my doctor this morning
and asked him if wearing tight
jeans would aggravate my sciatica.
He told me he had people dying
of cancer in his surgery and hung up.
So I rang him back and asked would
it be safe to re-heat a steak 'n kidney
pie from yesterday.

DATING

I always give a heil Hitler salute
on my first date and rant on about
badger baiting.
I never show my good side,
they always bugger off.

Sometimes I smack myself in the face,
refuse to buy a round, or talk about
life in a mental hospital.
I never show my good side,
they always bugger off.

But usually I just get steaming drunk
and talk of human scum – this one never
fails to alienate and send them on the run.

THOUGHT FOR THE DAY

I wish for once the day
would not begin
the night is not long
enough – it seems no time
at all and the birds start
their bloody twittering and
we're off again.

ALARM CALL

When I was eighteen
still living at home
I was awoken each morning
by the screams of a then
undiagnosed schizophrenic.
She'd run upstairs bang
on my door and ask me
what I wanted for my birthday.
Sometimes she'd ask me when
I thought I might die and go
away laughing.
My sister now lives on her own by the sea
and I have an alarm clock.

SCRATCHED CAR

Before terminating our friendship
he gave me a lecture.
I had to listen
he held the moral high ground.
I scratched his car you see:
used my keys and went right
around forming a circle almost.
I offered him a pair of scissors
and told him to cut the arm off
my new leather jacket but he
declined and continued with
his lecture – verbal psychopath.

MEN AND MOTHERS

Fussing cuddling
ironing my short pants
I can handle this jungle
Cos mum's about.

And when I get older
and mummy is dead
I'll find a substitute
to pat my head.

She'll not be like mum
but will have a nice bum
she'll fail all mum's tests
but will have nice breasts.

If she's disloyal, unlike Mama,
I'll get stinking in my local bar.
Then back home I'll throw a fit,
and knock the wench about a bit.

FOR TED HUGHES

The birds are migrating
– who gives a fuck ...

DISTURBED

A fire rages in my mind
– the inescapable torture
of an unresolved unforgiving
past that returns to haunt me.
Time does not and cannot heal
this festering wound which does
not abate and only a death, without
an afterlife to still remember will
kill this mortal flame of torment.

ILL AT EASE

I've always felt
uncomfortable on this planet
never quite at ease
forever looking over my shoulder
or checking my pulse
I don't know what it is
really but I just can't
get comfortable.

NOT CELEBRATING THE NEW DECADE

Didn't care to celebrate
maybe falling down the stairs
electrocuting myself losing
one or both parents getting
hit by a car – having my first operation.
No hugs for me at twelve o'clock
I sat in a dark room biting my nails.

Didn't care to celebrate my
relationship ending badly
my hair falling out getting
into debt some form of mental
illness my first suicide attempt
another world war.
No hugs for me at twelve o'clock
I sat in a dark room shaking
uncontrollably.

Didn't care to celebrate
losing my job getting
butted in a bar ominous pains
in my left arm and not prepared
to revel in future misfortunes
sat chain smoking in a dark room.
No hugs for me at twelve o'clock.

THE GREAT HUMAN FARCE

I love you
I hate your guts
You're so kind
You're a cruel bastard
Shall we start a family
I'm having custody of the kids
You're so exciting
You're no fun anymore
Will you make love to me
Don't even touch me
I want to be with you
I've found somebody else
I really care about you
Drop dead!

STRIVING FOR IMPERFECTION

Teach me to play the
game of life with all
its twisted rules.
Teach me positive thinking
that great human lie we
deceive ourselves with
in order to cope.
Help me to learn the
lie so I can survive too.

DIFFERENT KIND OF FATHER

My dad wanted
to be a priest
and my mum wanted
to be a housewife
and they fought like
cat and dog.
My dad called it
a pseudo marriage
– a con.
My mum called it
a disgrace.
They broke each other's
hearts and ours too.
We buried them together.

WIND UP

I was invited to dinner
by the vicar last week,
duck was mentioned.
I arrived on time with
a bottle of wine but he
did not answer the door.
I thought I saw the curtain move.

DEATH

Death is a Socialist
he comes to us all
the rich the smug
the mad and the small.

The reaper's a lefty
a decent sort
he doesn't take
Barclaycard
he shits on us all.

He mocks our plans
causes much pain
arrives unannounced
in horrible forms.

Yet for all his faults
he ends suffering
for many and sorts out
the smart arses
once and for all.
I take my hat off to him,
death the greatest leveller
for sure.

THE SECRET CRIER

The old man wept
privately making
sure the windows
were closed and
mortise lock was
on the front door.
He had been caught
crying once before
in the trenches on
the Somme and had
been threatened
with a .38 revolver.

HORRIBLE THOUGHT

As I sat talking to the girl I loved
I noticed an axe on the fire-hearth
and a most unpleasant thought flashed
through my mind. It made me feel ashamed
guilty and rather horrible. I turned my
chair round so as not to see the axe but
it remained in my mind and I felt even
worse even more guilty that the axe had
such an effect on me it had caused me
to move my chair so I moved it back again.
'What's with all the chair movements?' asked
my girlfriend. 'It's the axe isn't it?
I'll go and put it in the kitchen – out of
sight out of mind.'

C$_2$ H$_5$ OH

One or Two
I can't do
Three or Four
leads to more
Five or Six
I'm in a fix
Seven or Eight
lose a mate
Nine or Ten
never again
Anything over
nut-house in Dover.

HYPOCRITE

She said men are horrible –
they're sick they're violent
they start wars they kill easily
they're rough bullying domineering
tyrants, macho swines.
I agreed with her and said imagine
fancying one – how much sicker that would be.
She slapped my face and left – collaborator.

BRILLIANT STUDENT

Excelled in all subjects
a great sportsman
wonderful sense of humour
fell off a cliff.

Active in everything
lived life to the full
a generous nature
stabbed to death
at a disco.

A great guy
with a great future
cheerful and optimistic
head crushed in
a car crash.

Full of ideas
always dashing about
popular with the ladies
fell onto a javelin.

A kind heart
and sense of fairness
always fun to be with
inhaled his own vomit.

G.B.H.

I've pushed you off buildings
into trains and spikes
I've removed bits from
walls imagining your eyes
I've slashed pillows and
curtains butted doors
and shattered glass
I've done all this and more
Yet I still see you laughing
in a Glasgow bar.

NATURE POEM

This morning,
I observed from my bedroom window
two squirrels chasing each other –
from tree to tree they leapt but
it wasn't for my entertainment.
They had had a furious row which
had erupted into violence.
I suspect a woman may have been involved.

FIREMEN

Big fat sons of Satan
clumsy psychopaths
never on time.

Pathological liars
so full of hate
not a bit of compassion
never far from trouble.

Absolute cowards
obsessed with water
noisy buffoons
shouting about nothing.

Bone-idle incompetents
children in uniform
can start nothing
can only put things out.

The most corrupt
profession in the world
a job for sneaky
little shits and
greedy egomaniacs.

BEST SELLER

Poetry doesn't normally sell,
but mine might because I intend
to embark on a series of bizarre
motiveless murders on and around
Hampstead Heath. Poetry doesn't
normally sell, but mine might.

HURRY UP AND DIE

I wish more people
I know would die
I like a good funeral
and seldom cry.

How long must I
wait for them to die
I like a good drink and
a piece of pie.

GAMES WITH GRANDMA

Sometimes when my Gran
was sleeping I would have
fun tying her shoelaces
together or placing objects
on her head. One time I removed
her left eye with a bayonet.

WHEN DID YOU LAST SEE
YOUR FATHER?

Where's your father Paul?
Down south miss
What's he doing there?
Teaching miss
Why doesn't he teach
up here?
He likes the climate miss
When's he coming back?
Don't know miss
Why isn't he with
his family?
He can't stand us miss
Is that why you shake
your head?
Don't know miss
Alright sit down.

THE ROCK SHOP

We were always making fun
at the man in the Rock Shop.
Once he got very angry
and began throwing
his stock at us –
rare stones of varying
colours whizzed past our ears
and my friend was hit in the face
with a piece of malachite.
The police took him away
and his shop closed down.
Some weeks later he killed himself by
swallowing some pulverised granite.

CHEST PAINS AT 3am

There goes another speeding ambulance
without its siren on – a heart attack
case – they don't like to cause them
undue stress. But they cause me stress.
I imagine the poor sod lying on a settee
gasping for breath and chewing an aspirin
his frantic wife and kids looking on –
how much easier to die on your own.
I wonder when it will be my turn,
and ring an ambulance to see how
long it takes to arrive – they are
not amused.

WASTE OF TIME

First of all
you search for one.
Then you find you
like them but don't
fancy them.
You fancy them
but don't like them.
You fancy and like
them but they only
like you.
You fancy and like
them but they only
fancy you.
You fancy and like
them and they fancy
and like you – you
both fall in love
and in one to five
years one of you
fancies someone else
and it all ends sour.

ON LOSING A MOTHER
AT SIXTEEN

A bad age to lose a mother say some
psychologists – neither a boy nor
a man – a mere fledgling leaving
the nest. I was devastated – felt
lost, deserted even betrayed and
found it difficult to relate to
women for a long time after. I
wondered how I would fill all the
years of a life without her; although
as with my father's death some years
later it did give me a new sense of
freedom which I felt slightly guilty
about, but I don't think I could have
lazed around on the dole had she lived.
Like many immigrants she was obsessed
with her children's education and
sadly lived just long enough to learn
I'd failed most of my 'O' Levels.

ONSET OF MADNESS

One day my sister
quite suddenly, without warning
went mad.
I remember I was in the garden
at the time playing with a friend
when I heard this awful scream.
I thought someone had had an
accident and froze. But then
came the sound of laughter
followed by more screams
and then shouting from my father.
'What's happening in there' asked
my friend I said I didn't know.
Then suddenly the kitchen door
flung open and my sister ran into
the garden naked screaming at the
top of her voice with my father
chasing after her. He told me to
dial 999 and ask for an ambulance.
My friend left.

LIFE GOES ON

I dislike people
because they're
always getting
over things.
With such ease
they carry on
because they say
life must go on
but must it?
and is this really
the case or are they
just insensitive
miserable little
earthlings with
not much feeling
at all.

IMAGINE

Imagine if the only
way of dying was to
be kicked to death.
There would be thousands
of kickings every minute.
Every time you went out
to buy a newspaper you'd
see someone being kicked
to death; and you'd always
be wondering just when and
where and by whom you were
going to get your fatal kicking.

BARGAIN

My next door neighbour – strange woman,
smoked eighty Kensitas a day and collected
the coupons feverishly. I've saved enough
to buy a clock she said after having a lung
removed – I've just got a toaster she said
as her right leg came off. Will you collect
my portable television, she asked me as she
lay in hospital having had her third stroke
and a few years later as she lay dying what
seemed to upset her most was that she was
only ten points off a gorgeous mahogany coffin.

DEVASTATED

Yesterday I spent three hours
making a stew and then
dropped it on the carpet.
I was so upset
I rang the Police they
told me not to be so
stupid and asked me if
I lived on my own.

DEAD ERNEST

Ernest Hemingway
wasn't gay
but blew his brains out
anyway.

ENEMIES

I sometimes wonder what it would
be like to sit in a room full of
all the people who dislike me –
yet don't know each other – would
their common loathing of myself
unite them? Are they similar types
perhaps? Would they all get along?
And would I survive the experience?

HIGH PRICE

I only wanted a shag,
now I'm married with
three kids – working
all the hours God sends
and her mother stays most
weekends – wish I'd had
a wank instead.

PIGS AND SEX

Most people are ugly
and there's too much
sex about anyway – so
abstain you ugly fuckers
and leave sex to the good
lookers.

KILLING TIME

It's ten-thirty in the morning
and I sit and wonder if anyone
in the world has been bitten
by a snake yet.

Now it's eleven – surely someone
must have severed an artery by now
or died in the operating theatre.

Now it's twelve and I'm late for
my psychiatrist.

UNPLEASANT COMPANY

I had to ask him to stop
calling round in the end.
He kept treading in dog-dirt
and rubbing it into my carpet.
Once he brought a friend round
and he had stood in some too.
They both sat there smiling –
the living-room stank for days.

THE CORLETTS

They were three blonde sisters
and I liked them all, especially
Janet, even though my friend said
she had a face like a parrot.
I found her purple hat in the street
once and brought it round to the
house – she wasn't very friendly
and when I asked her would she go
out with me immediately said no
and shut the door in my face.
I was heart-broken she was the
first girl I had fallen unsuccessfully
in love with – looking back I suppose
she didn't like my unfashionable
scruffy appearance, not to mention
my weird friends and eccentric father.
But going out with her would have
helped me enormously in those dark
days of my sister's schizophrenia and
mother's premature death. I saw her
cleaning her front door knocker when
I was last up in Liverpool. I had a
poem in the Guardian that day and
thought of going over and showing it
to her, but I don't suppose it would
have done any good, not now anyway.

SHARED LETTER-BOX

Stealing people's mail
is fun to do
unless of course
they think it's you.

Money and chocolates
I've had them all
and none of them
addressed to Paul.

But be careful
when you play this game
in case your neighbours
do the same.

EDINBURGH

If it wasn't for the cars
on the streets you wouldn't
know what century you were in.
As it is I keep thinking I'm
going to be shot by a musket,
challenged to a duel or waylaid
by footpads.

PUBLIC HOUSES

Most boozers
are horrible places
full of losers
getting out of their faces.

Lounging on stools
letting the day slip by
talking with fools
whose only wish is to die.

They're a kind of home
albeit sad
for those all alone
and a little bit mad.

UNLIKELY POET

I told my sister I stuffed
a piece of fillet steak down
my trousers in the supermarket.
She said I bet Wordsworth wouldn't
have done that.

FOR YOUR THROAT'S SAKE
SMOKE CRAVEN A

I wish I could have been
a smoker before 1952 when
all the health scares started.
All that wonderful advertising –
doctors offering you one in the
surgery – smoking in cinemas on
buses and trains. No quitlines,
nicotine patches or warnings on
packets. No guilt worry or social
exclusion and costing much less too.
I wish I could have been a smoker
before 1952.

REPRESSED

He was so distressed when
he realised he was homosexual
he went to his local A and E.
An attractive nurse gave him
an injection of valium – he
tried to have a wank about her
when he got home.

NIGHTS
In memory of Philip Larkin

What are nights for?
nights are where we sleep,
they come, time and time
over. They are to be happy
in. Where can we sleep but
nights?

Ah, solving that question
brings the dentist and the
milkman in their underpants
running down the street.

POSITIVE DISCRIMINATION

There's a little restaurant
in Chiswick where there's a
ban on courting couples and
the waiters are in wheelchairs;
the food is very good.

JUST SHIT

People are tossers
become a hermit
and cut your losses.

COUNTING FOR MY LIFE

Sitting in my local pub
I find myself counting
the number of candles
on tables and imagine
they are the years I have
left to live. But seven
is not enough – so I stare
down at the floor and count
the number of discarded fag ends –
though nine is still too short –
so I turn my attention to the spirit
bottles behind the bar and with some
relief count fourteen – that's more like it.

LAST MEAL

He had always enjoyed his food
so it was a hard decision what
to choose, and indeed he changed
his mind some twenty-five times
keeping the prison chef up all night.
He finally went for a traditional
English breakfast which he threw up
on his way to the death chamber.

ARTISTIC STATEMENT

Although he had paid for my book
and it was entirely up to him what
he did with it, I was still annoyed
when he started to bend the thing
while talking to me, so I told him to stop.
He responded by tearing the cover off
then folding it into four and stuffing
it in his back pocket.

WATCHING THE BOX

It's not dying I so much mind
but everyone watching the box –
my box – staring, imagining –
recalling their own particular
moments with me, and me not being
able to communicate, rest or even
die with such a concentrated force
of eyes watching me. And at the burial
too – all eyes on me again – then the
wake – everyone talking about me and
in my flat – is there no peace?
No, I'll have to wait until they spout
that famous cliché life goes on, and
then forget about me.

ODD BEHAVIOUR

Just recently I've taken to putting
up two fingers at funeral cortèges,
and have been beaten up several times.
My Psychiatrist tells me it's just a
phase I'm going through – a kind of
mid-life crisis, not unusual for a
man of my age and background. I asked
him was it common, and he said in some
parts of India it occurs quite a lot
and referred me to the School of Tropical
Medicine.

FOUR TIMES A YEAR

It's always the same
Man drowns trying to save dog
Siege in East London
Travel chaos
Girl abducted
Just another Bank Holiday.

PERIOD

How strange to see Victorians
in old photographs in the prime
of life, walking around with
such confidence and self-assurance,
sometimes with their children,
who are also dead.

SUMMER-TIME BLUES

It's here again, hot weather and flies,
long days, another football tournament
– how I hate it.

Picnics in the park, men with no shirts on
exposing sickly white skin – everyone wearing
stupid bright shorts.

Kids running amok in beer gardens,
fear of swallowing a wasp, pressure
to go on holiday – sweating like a pig.

Stinking tennis, noisy transistors,
weird things growing, not enough darkness
– talking shit at barbecues.

Laughing couples holding hands, old people
moaning, can't sleep at night and to round
it all off that three day nightmare – The
Notting Hill Carnival.

I don't think I can take another one of these
– let me die in March please.

PERFECT REVENGE

Although he was very experienced in First Aid
and knew the Heimlich Technique very well,
he still refused to perform the manoeuvre
when his old Headmaster began choking
on a piece of meat at their annual reunion dinner.
He later explained to the Police that he quite
simply didn't like the guy – no charges were
brought.

THE PAST

I always prefer the past –
last year, last month,
last week, yesterday,
five minutes ago.
The past is a safer place
to be – to hang out in;
and you don't die.

BEHIND CLOSED DOORS

I've started a graffiti war in the toilet
of my local pub. It began innocently enough
with a short political statement, but now
it's turned quite unpleasant. Several people
appear to be involved judging by the different
handwriting and various threats have been made,
as well as an insulting drawing of myself depicting
me as a snake. The Landlady has tried painting
it over a couple of times, but it just starts up again
with increasing nastiness. She's now thinking of
bringing the Police in, as the atmosphere in the pub
is quite tense.

2/8/12 – 12.15pm   CAN YOU HELP?

The street is quiet again now,
the morbid onlookers have gone
about their business. The wreckage
cleared – the blood cleaned up –
the motorcyclist dead. A young
couple kiss near the tragic spot
unaware of the fatal accident which
occurred earlier. The icecream man
arrives, but no-one leaves their
house to buy one – it is a hot day
and he can't understand why. In
another part of the city a police
car moves slowly up the road of
the deceased man's parents.

BENEFIT KING

When I grow up I'm going to be
an astronaut a footballer a physicist
or be long term unemployed.

When I grow up I'm going to be
a rock star an actor a politician
or be long term unemployed.

When I grow up I'm going to be
a doctor a lawyer a fireman
or be long term unemployed.

When I grow up I'm going to be
an architect a marine biologist a painter
or be long term unemployed.

When I grow up I'm going to climb
Mt Everest invent things run my own business
or be long term unemployed.

When I grow up I'm going to have a beautiful wife
three lovely children a big house and flash car
or be long term unemployed.

NEAR LIFE EXPERIENCE

I stopped keeping a diary
it was getting embarrassing
I had nothing to write about
and somebody might have found it.

PARANOID

He checked every new book
of poetry that came out
and every magazine to see
if anyone had stolen his poems.
He was obsessed with plagiarism,
then someone mentioned translations –
what about translations? and unable
to cope with the idea drove his
bubble car over a cliff.

SINGLE

Last Friday night I got chased
by celibate-bashers in Camden Town.
They caught up with me outside the
tube station – called me an 'abstaining
bastard' and gave me one hell of a kicking.
The Police say it's a new type of 'hate crime'
which they haven't encountered before
but are taking very seriously.

NIGHTMARE

Imagine waking up and discovering you were a fascist
having to ring all your friends and tell them you hate
blacks and jews – want to restore capital punishment
and send queers and gypsies to special camps.
Imagine waking up and realizing you were a fascist –
having to attend nasty meetings full of odious
characters, put racist stickers on lampposts and
give your local asian councillor abusive phone calls
in the middle of the night. Imagine it – feeling
bitter and twisted inside – what on earth would you do
if you really believed it? See your local doctor?
But he's a paki too.

A MEMORY OF LIVERPOOL

His name was Jimmy – horrible little man,
got cancer of the throat at forty-two
and survived – one of a very small group
I believe. He used to say the best
way of injuring someone in a pub
was to wait until they put a glass
to their lips and then give it a hard
shove. Even now when a stranger approaches
me in a bar I'm quick to remove the glass
from my mouth.

AT THE VET

'What's your cat's name?'
    'Tinker'

'What's his date of birth?'
    '2nd of April 98'

'What's his National Insurance number?'
    'What?'

'Has he ever been a member of a trade union?'
    'No'

'Has he ever been a member of the Communist Party?'
    'Not to my knowledge'.

TOO GOOD

I was putting the cat's
lunch out today – delicious
chunks of rabbit and liver
in a rich gravy. It looked
so nice I decided to eat it
myself and gave Tinker an
apple instead.

A DYING MAN'S THOUGHTS

Will I outlive this new extra large
bottle of sauce?
Will I outlive the giant box of tea bags
my sister brought round?
Will I outlive this mega tube of toothpaste
or the light bulb I've just fitted?
Should I buy this bottle of orange squash?
Will I be able to finish it? Or will it
outlive me?

LIVING DANGEROUSLY

I once met a man in a café
who said the life experience
was not in the slightest bit
dangerous – even the first world
war he exclaimed wasn't dangerous,
and he had a relative who survived
the Titanic. He also said he never
watched the news or bought papers,
but I noticed he was carrying a knife,
and I took an extra valium before going
to bed that evening, and slept peacefully
through the great storm of eighty-seven.

LET'S HEAR IT FOR THE MENTALLY ILL!

They don't push you around
or sleep with your wife.
They don't enter politics
or refuse you a smoke.
Let's hear it for the mentally ill!

They don't have big egos
or drive fast cars.
They don't go jogging
or play five a side.
Let's hear it for the mentally ill!

They don't travel abroad
or dress up smart.
They don't become famous
or compete in any way.
Let's hear it for the mentally ill!

They don't attend weddings
or have much fun.
They don't have children
or live that long.
Let's hear it for the mentally ill!

FRIEND OR FOE?

Are we naturally horrible?
Is it just easier to be nice
to each other?
Is it all just an act?
Do we really want to kill
each other?
Mother, brother, lover,
and is this niceness
just a cover?
Friend or foe?
I'd like to know.

PSYCHOTIC EPISODE

They must have thought I was Martin Luther
reincarnated when I walked into the church
that evening, having not slept for five days,
and began knocking all the candles off the altar,
and decked the Prior who tried to stop me.
Then later when three of them were restraining
me in the sacristy – calling them the Inquisition.
Well they were Dominicans, formerly the Black Friars,
and looked quite intimidating in their hooded robes.
The one I hit, like a good Christian visited me
in hospital the following week – he looked a bit uneasy
when I got up off my bed suddenly to light a cigarette.

SUICIDE

One of the advantages of committing suicide
is that you can choose a relatively painless
and dignified death. Yet it often amazes me
the grotesque methods some people use,
like jumping in front of a tube train –
What's that all about? The traumatized driver
gets a week off work and the tubes are disrupted
for hours. Slashing one's wrists isn't much better –
what a bloody mess. I once knew someone who jumped
off a block of flats when all the kids were coming
home from school – he didn't die immediately.

HUMILIATED

He killed both his parents
and his sister, as well as
a neighbour and the local priest.
Sentenced to life in prison – in
his first year he killed a fellow
inmate and a guard. The subject of
a television documentary some years
later, when asked by the interviewer
what he would do if he was released,
he said he'd 'kill more humans'.
His Psychiatrist attributed much of
his behaviour to an incident which
occurred when he was at Primary School,
when a female class-mate beat him in
a playground fight and sat on his face.
He went berserk afterwards, smashing windows
and assaulting staff.

MID-LIFE CRISIS

'But doctor, look at my hands,
just look at them, they're all wrinkled.'
'Well, you're nearly fifty. What do you expect?'
was the unsympathetic reply.
'But I haven't lived! I haven't bloody lived!'
he exclaimed, tears rolling down his face.
'Well, that's not my fault. Would you like
a prescription for some hand cream or perhaps
an anti-depressant?'

9/11

He'd been unhappy for a long time,
and had been planning his suicide
for months. So he was the first
to jump from the World Trade Centre
that day, even before the fire had
taken hold. A short note was found
on his body – it read 'This suicide
is entirely my own fault, no-one else
is to blame at all.'

NOVEMBER 22nd – LONDON

It never really got light today,
I've seen days like it before
this time of year. But the leaves
they are so beautiful this autumn,
such unusual colours; we should be
grateful to the Victorians, strange
though they were, for planting so many
trees, it must have taken their minds
off sex – poor souls.

GLOBAL WARMING

It was snowing when I woke
this morning and was sunny
at midday. There was a party
having their Christmas dinner
in the pub and I got stung by
a bloody great bee – all this
in mid-February. I've also
noticed those old guys with
'THE END IS NIGH' signboards
seem a lot more confident
these days – have a certain
spring in their step.

ALCOHOLIC

I often talk to strangers in bars,
and sometimes wonder what it would
be like to meet my late parents –
out for a drink together in their
early courting days. Would I bore
them too? Ruin their evening perhaps?
I can almost hear them saying – 'What
a sad lonely man' as they hurriedly leave,
though I prefer to think of them as being
polite and kind.

NINETY-TWO IS THE NEW EIGHTEEN

Some deluded and pathetic middle-class
lovers of life are beginning to say
that seventy is the new fifty, it's
not true of course, they are really
very old and are going to die quite soon,
some of them in a lot of pain.

DISILLUSIONED POET

I'm organizing a book burning
bonfire next summer at Hay-on-Wye,
for all the poetry no-one wants to buy.

PSYCHIATRIC WARD

I enter the TV lounge with usual apprehension
and sit next to an attractive new arrival.
I tell her I like her dress, she looks away
in disgust and mutters something about
sticking a pen in my eye. I get a cold feeling
in my stomach and change seats. 'The Terminator'
is on TV and although people stare in that direction,
nobody is really watching it. Then one patient
gets up suddenly and pushes the television over.
Somebody shouts and a brief argument ensues,
but the set is broken – terminated! Everyone
carries on staring at the vacant space.
A big lady in a pink dressing-gown and one slipper
starts laughing – she calls us all devil worshippers
and leaves the smoke-filled room. I smell food,
it's nearly lunch-time and I'm starving, a side effect
of the medication. I've put on half a stone since I've
been here. Then the alarm goes off (third time today).
Nurses run to guard the exit. I haven't got enough
cigarettes.

SMASH POSITIVE THINKING!

Smash positive thinking
show it up for the filthy cheap
lie that it is.
It's this filth – this wicked
con – this vile perverted form
of self-deceit that has kept
this foul planet with its
depraved wretched souls in
a confused state of optimistic
misery and torture for over
two thousand years.
Smash positive stinking thinking
for it and it alone is the cause
of our continuous suffering,
our hopeless and most unsatisfactory
existence. Smash it now, this minute.
Refuse to think positively. After all
why should you have to?

SHITE

In the beginning there was shite
followed by more shite
followed by even more shite
until there was just shite

MY CLOSE SHAVE WITH CANCER

I met him outside the hospital
crying in his pyjamas. 'I've got cancer'
he said – 'fuckin' cancer! Would you believe it –
Me! Who's never smoked a cigarette in his life!
Six months to live – fuckin' lung cancer.
You should have it the way you smoke, not me –
Why don't you have fuckin' cancer!' I told him
I was very sorry; at which point he turned nasty.
'It's all your fault' he said, 'Chain-smoking in the
pub all the time – you gave me the fuckin' cancer!'
'Now hold on' I said, 'You can't blame me for your
filthy stinking cancer.' 'Oh yes I can' he roared,
and began strangling me; but I managed to break
free and ran away – My close shave with cancer.

GRAND NATIONAL DAY

I met him in the street,
and asked him if he was putting a bet on.
'No I can't' he said, 'I'm a vegetarian'.
What's that got to do with it I thought –
people have always got to be something.
I remember the year the IRA disrupted
the race, and the horses watched while
all the people ran.

FIFTIES

My dad finally came home from his travels
when he was fifty – home to an unhappy marriage
with six kids who didn't like him very much.
I don't recall him having any friends either,
nor did he drink or smoke, and he hated his job
at the City Analysts, where he was bypassed for
promotion in favour of younger men. He used to
get up very early when no-one was around, and
pretend to go to sleep on the sofa each night
after tea. Even at the age of seven I could tell
he was unhappy – it was as if it was all over for him.
I think it must have been his worst decade. He died
at seventy-three.

ARNOLD HEAD

He was my Clinical Psychologist
for the best part of a year when
I was twenty – GP referral.
I mostly talked about my childhood,
but he wasn't very interested –
seemed to think I wasn't a serious case.
Once he fell asleep when I was recounting
a particularly traumatic incident –
even started snoring. His last advice
to me was to get myself a girlfriend.
'It will take your mind off things'
he said, chewing peanuts.

SMOKING IN THE CINEMA

I used to like going to the cinema
with my father on a Friday night,
but hated the arguments he always
had with smokers. 'It causes lung
cancer you know' he'd turn round
and say. 'You'll have heart disease
by the time you're fifty.' They always
told him to shut up! and on one occasion
set fire to his hood.

WAR IN THE HOME

I was late wearing my white peace poppy
that year, and got the usual hostile glances.
But one rather nervous old man stopped me
in the street nearly in tears. He told me
his father had been a conscientious objector
in the war, but had battered his mother to death
with a hammer. 'I think he was very violent under
the surface' he said, 'but would have approved
of your poppy.'

WONDERFUL

I've heard of these charismatic
charming types, full of kindness
and love, and the trail of misery
and hurt they leave behind them.
Give me the odious and cynical
instead, they harm no-one ultimately,
and always sleep in a single bed.

SHOPLIFTING

I'm always pilfering small items –
my motto is anything that fits in
the pocket goes in the pocket.
I save a small fortune shopping this way.
Last week the manager of my supermarket
told me there was a special offer on the fish.
I felt like saying there is on the cheese too,
it's in my pocket. I expect to get caught soon,
but I'm a grand ahead easy.

TWISTED HEAD

'How's your boyfriend?' I asked.
'He twisted my head to 360 degrees'
she said, 'tried to kill me – twisted
my head to 360 degrees – he's army trained.'
'Why did he do that?' 'I don't know. He just
grabbed hold of my head and twisted it right round.'
'To 360 degrees?' 'Yes to 360 degrees. It felt like
it was going to come off.'

UNCLE FRED

My dad was very morbid
and I remember when I was ten
and had to have four teeth out
at the dentist, overhearing him
telling my mother in the kitchen
that I was having a major operation,
and that was how uncle Fred went, in
the dentist's chair in 1935. It sent a
shiver down my spine and,terrified
at the prospect of going like uncle
Fred, I stayed awake all night, and
when the dentist told me there was
nothing to worry about I felt like
saying you don't know about uncle Fred,
and when I came round after the anaesthetic
I was overjoyed to be alive and not to have
gone like uncle Fred.

DODGY

I realized I was in bad company
when one of the group dropped a
tenner, and his mate put his foot
on it, then slipped it into his pocket.
He ordered a double from the bar,
and bought crisps for everyone.

THE COLONEL'S DINNER

I know this black girl
who's obsessed with Kentucky
fried chicken. Every time I
meet her she sez 'I can't stop
I'm going to get the colonel's dinner.'
I met her in the pub and she tried to
borrow money. 'I'm a bit short for the
colonel's dinner' she said. Last week
I met her in the supermarket. 'You must
come round for a meal' she said, 'I'll
get the colonel's dinner.' It was then
I snapped. 'Will you shut up about the
colonel's stinking dinner' I said, 'It's
crap, and the colonel is a racist bigot
and a white supremacist.' She looked slightly
dismayed and said 'I think I'll get coleslaw
instead of beans with the colonel's dinner tonight.'

TOO MUCH

She is mentally ill
and was feeding the pigeons
in the street when a car spun
round the corner and squashed
one of them. She got blood on
her shoe – it hasn't been an
easy life.

REQUIRED READING

I often stay at a writers' retreat
in Reigate – a place frequented by
various academics and intellectuals.
It has a great library full of all
the classics, but I always bring
something light to read – like
Wind in the Willows, Swallows and
Amazons or a John Creasey thriller.
My choice of reading has often been
ridiculed by other guests and one
said recently – why don't you just
bring a colouring book?

DEATH ON THE SLAB

I've never liked the idea
of dying in the operating theatre –
all the panic and pandemonium –
doctors shouting, nurses rushing
about – we're losing him, we're
losing him! I've seen it so often
on television – such an undignified
and chaotic end. I was therefore
surprised when I met a theatre nurse
recently, who told me none of this
was the case. He had experienced
death in the operating theatre a
number of times and said there was
just calm, calm and real sadness.

THE POUND NOTE

There was a brief period in the sixties
when my dad was out of work and had no money.
He sold my old push-bike to a neighbour for
a pound. It seemed like such a lot then and
I remember he was very reluctant to break into it –
it was like the last pound note in the world;
but when he finally did for a round of ice creams,
it seemed to last forever.

SMOKING ON THE TRAIN

Not being able to smoke on long-distance
train journeys is a real inconvenience.
I always have at least one in the toilet.
Coming back from Edinburgh last year everyone
was at it, including someone with a pipe.
The guard went mad and kept warning us
over the intercom. Finally he said the police
were getting on at Crewe to escort all the smokers
off the train. He was bluffing of course.
He could smell us, but he couldn't see us.

REVENGE

He ripped my manky old Afghan coat
in a bit of horseplay outside the pub
and in revenge I lifted his brand new
designer leather jacket and sold it to
a student. I heard he was devastated by
its loss and offered a reward for its
return. I think he knew it was me and
when I met him some years later after
he had become a born-again Christian,
seemed over-friendly, like he was making
a point that he'd forgiven me.

PHONE A FRIEND

For a devout Catholic,
he was in no hurry to meet his maker,
I suspect we're all agnostic at heart.
He saw his GP twice a week, who eventually
said to him – 'You think if you keep seeing
the doctor you won't die.' But old age is
of course the biggest killer and he was eighty-six.
Because of a morbid fear of being buried alive,
he insisted his mobile phone be put in his coffin.
I tried calling him, but the reception was bad.
I hope he had some credit left on his phone.

GEOFFREY MILLER

The Landlord's name over the door
said Geoffrey Miller licensed to sell
beer, wines and intoxicating spirits –
so in we went. 'Are you Geoffrey Miller?'
I said to a bald fat man with a small
moustache. 'Yes' he replied. 'Would that
be the same Geoffrey Miller licensed
to sell beer, wines and intoxicating spirits?'
'It is indeed' he said looking slightly proud
of himself. 'Right we'll have some of that'
I said and we both sat down, and for several
hours consumed everything Geoffrey Miller
could throw at us. Finally I fell off my stool,
and my friend threw up on the bar, at which point
Geoffrey Miller turned nasty and refused to sell us
any more of his beer, wines, or intoxicating spirits,
and threatened to call the Police if we didn't leave.
So we said 'Fuck you Geoffrey Miller!' and left.

PSYCHOPATH

He bought my poetry book
for the full price and got
me to sign it to 'Killer',
his nine year old pitbull
terrier with a long fighting
pedigree. I saw him stamp on
somebody's face in the pub once,
and wondered if I should have
given him one free. He said
he liked the one about fear the best.

THE LIE

My sister phones me from her allotment,
I tell her Prince Charles is dead –
polo accident, Windsor Great Park.
She is shocked – tells everyone on
the allotment. She goes home, there's
no mention of it on the news. Finds
out he's not dead. Next time she's
on the allotment, she gets weird looks,
and no-one speaks to her.

MAD FRANKIE

He must have been in this thirties –
rode a push-bike and wore goggles
and a motor-bike helmet – had Hell's
Angels and Live to Ride, Ride to Live
scrawled on the back of his denim cut-off
in red biro ink. He would cycle furiously
around the streets, swearing at passers-by
and giving the V-sign. I think the poor fellow
was soft in the head and the figure of much
amusement in the neighbourhood – harmless though.
I don't know what became of him, just one of the
many faces I no longer see when I go home.

EYES

I sometimes worry just how easy
it is to blind oneself – a simple
prick from a cocktail stick or sewing
needle, a little jab from your ball-point
pen, or a gentle shove with your house key –
blinded in an instant with the slight flick
of a wrist, never to see again – a lifetime
of darkness, because of one act of madness.
I sometimes worry how easy it is to blind oneself.

SHE MUST HAVE DREAMT
ABOUT ME

She must have dreamt about me,
as I so often have dreamt about her,
and felt sad for a moment when she awoke –
genuinely missed me – wanting to spend
the day in my company – laughing and
walking on Primrose Hill.

THE LOUNGE

I remember when pubs used to have
lounges and public bars. The lounges
were always a bit more expensive.
I remember asking a publican once
why this was. 'You're standing on
carpet' he said.

FIRST DATE

The first time a girl ever rang
me up was really embarrassing.
My father answered and got very
excited. He started shouting 'It's
a girl for Paul – a girl for Paul'
and then dropped the phone causing
a big crash. I had to pretend he was
drunk.

LONELINESS

If you were to somehow bottle
this awful feeling and then
drink it down, it would make
you very ill – eight bottles
of the stuff – a gallon of
loneliness might even kill you –
to drown in loneliness, pure undiluted
loneliness – a horrible agonizing death.

REST IN PEACE

When I die I hope it's in the winter,
instead of the summer – to quietly
slip away on a cold dark February
morning would suit me fine, rather
than going in the mad frenzy of mid-summer –
long hot days, bright sunshine, people
laughing about my death in shorts.

JUST AROUND THE CORNER

Trying to enjoy my time here
before the bad things happen,
and they will – all kinds of
wondrous delights – X-rays,
scans, dialysis and operations.
Hip replacements, strokes and cancer.
Arthritis, heart bypass and dementia,
it's all waiting for me. You don't get
off that easily, you don't get off this
rotten planet without a whole load of
stinking pain. Trying to enjoy my time
here before the bad things happen.

DATES

I'm always looking at the dates
on newspapers, just to know I'm
alive at this moment in time.
I suppose if I was resurrected –
came back to earth after death –
the first thing I'd do would be
to look at a newspaper, check the
day, month and year – see how long
I'd been dead.

WHO'S WHO

Father Michael was explaining
to me how we won't have our bodies
in heaven, just our souls and I said
how will we recognize everyone – know
who we're talking to – Jesus Christ or
Bernard Manning, St Peter or Walt Disney,
John the Baptist or John Wayne, Francis
of Assisi or Enoch Powell, Mahatma Gandhi
or Fred Astaire, Mother Teresa or Lucille Ball?
Stop it! Stop it! You'll know, he said, you'll
just know.

BEDTIME

Last night, out of sheer boredom
I went to bed at 7 o'clock.
It felt odd drawing the curtains
when it was still light. I had not
been to bed at this time since I was eight.
But life was so much more fun then, I had
plenty to do. In fact I always wanted to
stay up late, nine or ten, sleeping was so dull,
but now it's the highlight of my day – how things
have changed. Last night I went to bed at 7 o'clock,
adult life has been something of a disappointment.

OUR BACK GARDEN

It wasn't very big, just a small
patch of grass really, but we all
loved our garden and enjoyed the
seasons in it. My mother, who had
lived on a farm grew plants and flowers,
and we had a cat, a rabbit, two tortoises
and some frogs we could never find. In summer
we would all sit out on deckchairs, drink chilled
orange squash, sunbathe and read books. There was
also a coal-shed and a lavatory where we kept tools,
and a statue of the sacred heart without a head in
the corner, which my dad had found on Formby beach.
Beyond it was a disused railway embankment – a massive
jungle of trees and thick long grass. We were all very
thankful for it though, our little garden – our first
contact with nature.

CITY LIFE

Being an urban poet,
I didn't write any poems
when I visited the Lake District.
Even walking round Wordsworth's
cottage and seeing his beautiful
garden where he wrote 'Daffodils'
didn't inspire me. No, only when
I got back to London and saw a
car accident did I start writing again.

NEW YEAR

I haven't seen in New Year for a long time,
I must be getting old. It used to be really
important to be somewhere at midnight – get
drunk, hug another human being; not so now.
I'm normally in bed by ten, but get woken up
by the fireworks – have a small whisky and
wish the cat all the best.

UNEMPLOYED

Nobody had any money in those days,
we got by borrowing off each other's giro.
Then someone mentioned in the pub that
you got fifty pounds cash if you donated
your body to medical science after death,
and a whole gang of us trooped up to the
medical school to enquire. 'We've stopped
doing that now,' we were told. Too many people
were registering in Liverpool. 'Have you thought
about joining the army?' said the woman with a
wry smile on her face.

SPRING IN LIVERPOOL

That spring my friend Rhino got a new bike,
a chopper with big fat wheels. He took it
to the Oxo park nearby and rode through all
the flower-beds, uprooting and scattering the
newly sprung daffodils and tulips – a mean and
callous act I thought. The old park-keeper with
his bad leg let out a yell of absolute pain and
tried to catch my friend, but was too slow;
later on I saw him crying through the window of his hut.

CONGO MEN

There was much conflict
in the Congo when I was
a child and whenever I
misbehaved my mother would
say the Congo men would get me.
It was something in the word Congo
that terrified me. They never did
get me, not yet anyway, even though
I live in London.

SHAVING

I can still remember the smell
of my father shaving and the little
red bag he kept his open razor in.
But he never shaved much under his chin,
and there was always a bit of stubble on
his neck which he used the scissors on.
I often wondered if he feared cutting
his own throat – perhaps he wanted to?

UNCLE JOE

He had once been in the IRA
and was interned for a while,
later joining a closed religious
order, only to leave when they
got a colour television set –
said he couldn't see the point anymore.
Then he turned up in Kilburn, North London,
working in a knicker factory. I met him on
the High Road one morning, he had a black eye
and seemed a bit drunk. 'I got jumped by Orange
bastards' he said. 'Don't tell my family you've
seen me, they think I'm dead.'

RUGBY MATCH

I had been avoiding contact
with the ball all season,
when to my surprise and horror
it landed straight in my arms,
and thirty or so testosterone-filled
young men charged towards me shouting.
I should have run for it – gone for a try,
but instead almost instinctively I threw
it high up in the air. 'It's not a hot potato'
roared an irate sports master. I suppose I did
make the game look a bit ridiculous.

THIS FEELS RIGHT

I'm surprised when I think how easily
I settled into the life experience as
a child – accepted everything. I mean
nothing unsettled me – the sky, the sun
and moon, seasons changing – even people
seemed natural enough. Washing, eating,
laughing, crying, our gorgeous tabby cat,
all seemed perfectly normal. It was almost
as if I'd been here before. Then I started
school and everything changed.

NOISE POLLUTION

I often shout and swear
at passing ambulances with
their siren on. They look
a bit perplexed, but it's
such a horrendous noise
we've imported from America,
goes right through you – an
assault on the senses; although
I am well aware that one day if
I'm in need, it might be the nicest
and most welcoming sound I ever hear.

WEIRDO

It was one of those perfect
summer evenings with a bright
full moon, which you could see
clearly through the toilet window.
'Have you seen the moon tonight?'
I said to the guy next to me.
'I don't want any funny business'
he replied.

LAST DAY

None of the teachers who taught us
were around that final afternoon at
Grammar School – probably frightened
of being assaulted after giving us so
much grief for five years, no more of
that though. We sat around unsupervised,
playing cards and smoking a bit and then
it seemed so simple, so absurdly easy to
just walk down the drive and out of the front
gate for the last time.

RECENTLY DECEASED

I was glad I'd left school
when my mother died. I would
have hated hearing the Headmaster
announce it at morning assembly,
everyone pitying me and being a
little nicer to me that day –
the class bully offering me a sweet,
being allowed to go first in the dinner queue

LIVERPOOL 8

The cosmopolitan bohemian quarter,
and also a red-light district –
my Catholic father hated it. He drove
us all through it once on the way to
somewhere and accelerated like mad.
'Don't look out the window' he shouted,
his face all screwed up. I was only eight
and hadn't a clue what was happening, but
I was intrigued and eventually got a flat
round there myself when I left home.
My father never came to visit.

OUTSIDE LAVATORY

I had to laugh when my poor schoolmate
used to defend their outside lav –
'It's more hygienic' he would say –
'No smells in the house and you use
an umbrella when it's raining.'
He didn't have a father.

THE HERMIT

And then there was the time my father
decided we should all see a hermit,
so we took a bus out to Freshfield
and called on this old chap who had been
in the first world war and afterwards
had built a small house on Freshfield beach.
He opened the door and we all stared at him,
then my father produced a camera and took his picture.
The hermit lunged at my father and we all ran away.

RETRACING ONE'S STEPS

When I was a child out walking,
I had this annoying habit of
stopping dead in my tracks,
then I'd walk back a bit,
turn and walk on again.
I did this to relive the feeling
of a moment before. Nobody ever
noticed or said anything.

NOT MISTER JONES!

My father was always arguing
and falling out with people
in the neighbourhood, but when
he clashed with Mister Jones,
our friendly cheerful greengrocer,
I remember my brother shouting in dismay,
'Oh not Mister Jones as well!'

NO INTEREST

I popped into my local library
and asked the staff if their stamper
was working properly. 'Yes it is' said
the woman, 'Why do you ask?' 'Because
no-one's borrowing my book.' 'Well that's
poetry' she said.

QUICK EXIT

It's typical really,
I haven't been invited to a party
for twenty years and when I finally
get to one they're all in their seventies
and eighties, except the vicar who was twenty-two.
The host kept saying 'The girls haven't arrived,
the girls haven't arrived,' and then they did –
all on sticks, which they tapped on the floor
as the vicar did a strange solo dance to 'Tragedy'
by the BeeGees.

TIME PLEASE

'Do you have the right time?'
he asked, 'It's about two-thirty'
I said. 'No I want the right time,
it has to be right.' He seemed agitated.
'Sorry I don't know.' 'Listen don't mess
me around on the time front will you, I
half killed a man once for doing that.'
Time to walk away.

DEAD AND BURIED

It's funny to think of Larkin dead
after all the things he said –
that poor wretched and fearful man –
if he could manage it anyone can.

HOW WAS IT FOR YOU?

If I was to meet up with people
in the afterlife, I should talk
about death and dying. How theirs
had been – get them to describe their
final moments. I should want to know
what it was like to fall from a high
building, die in a fire, get stabbed
or shot. I should want to hear from
those who drowned, hanged themselves,
bled to death, died of shock – soldiers
who were blown to bits in wars, folk that
died in car accidents, victims of poison
and torture. And of course those lucky ones
who passed away in their sleep – did they really
not feel a thing?

DOOR-TO-DOOR CANVASSING

'Don't come round here talking
about double glazing when my
wife's just died' he said.
'She might have wanted you to have it sir'
I replied, 'Keep yourself warm on those
cold nights without her.' 'What the hell
are you talking about' he yelled and chased
me down the garden path.

PROSTITUTE

I needed a few drinks
before I even rang her
and then my coin got stuck,
but I eventually got through.
I asked her did she have any
diseases and she said 'all of them!'
and hung up. I rang back immediately
and apologized – said I was inexperienced,
but she hung up again. I waited a bit then
tried one last time and a man answered so
I hung up, ripped up her card and went back
to my bedsit. I needed a bath anyway.

LOSING FRIENDS THROUGH DRINK

My old cat doesn't approve of my drinking.
He knows even when I've just had a few –
can hear my uneven steps on the stairs
and spot my quirky movements in the flat,
and when I try to stroke him he lashes out
aggressively and hisses. I think he'd like
me to go back to AA.

TROUBLE

'You've had a troubled life
and have a troubled mind,'
said the Psychotherapist.
'But I can't work with you,
it would be too much trouble.'

2016

My cat has just turned eighteen
and is now old enough to vote,
drink and fight. But sadly he is
dying, although eighteen is quite
an age for a cat, not so for a human,
and I am reminded that, exactly one hundred
years ago, thousands of eighteen-year-olds were
killed in one day during the battle of the Somme
– all of them no older than my cat.
They didn't get nine lives.

AUGUST

I always feel a sense of relief
when August comes – last month
of summer, autumn around the corner.
At last I can see the dark at the end
of the tunnel.

Those poems previously published in book form
are selected by the author from his collections
   Terrifying Ordeal
   So Far So Bad
   Rats Getting Close
   Odd Behaviour
   Willing to Change
   Do Not Disturb
   Collected Poems (2010)
   Required Reading (2012)
all published by Hearing Eye,
and from the pamphlets
   Smoking in the Cinema (2011)
   Rest in Peace (2014)
   You Should be Dead! (2016)
produced by SEM Publishing.

PAUL BIRTILL was born in Walton, Liverpool in 1960. He moved to London in his early twenties and, apart from a brief period in Glasgow, has lived there ever since. His poems appear regularly in national newspapers and literary magazines, and he has read on national radio and at poetry venues nationwide. He is also an accomplished playwright; several of his plays have been staged at London theatres, including *Squalor*, short-listed for the Verity Bargate Award.